Everybody
Masturbates

by
Cristian YoungMiller

Illustrated by
Andrew Toutant

RateABull
Books

The characters and events in this book are fictitious. Any similarity to real persons, living or dead, is coincidental and not intended by the author.

RateABull Books
Visit our Web site at www.RateABull.com

Book Design by Cristian YoungMiller
Illustrations by Andrew Toutant

ISBN-13: 978-0-982-71322-8
ISBN-10: 0-9827132-2-3

To everyone that was made to feel like they were the only ones doing it.

Boys masturbate.
Girls masturbate.
Monkeys masturbate.
Dogs masturbate.

Some people start to masturbate when they're very young. Some people start to masturbate when they're very old. Some people imagine themselves when they masturbate. Some people look at pictures of others when they masturbate.

There are people that masturbate in their bedroom and others in the bathroom. There are people that masturbate outside and others in planes… but that's not good.

Some people only use their hands when they masturbate and some people just their fingers. Some people use toys when they masturbate and others even use food.

There are people that masturbate in their dreams and others while they sleep. There are people that haven't done it since they were a kid and others that do it six times a day.

But no matter when you start and where you do it, one thing is certainly true--everybody masturbates. And as long as you respect yourself and others, masturbation is fun to do.

1

Billy wasn't feeling happy. In fact, since having an argument with his older brother Tommy, he had been lying on his bed crying. Billy's mom poked her head into Billy's bedroom. But when she asked what was wrong, Billy just turned away and said, "I want to speak to daddy."

In a few minutes Billy's dad came in, walked right over to Billy's bed, and

plopped himself down like he usually did.

"What's the matter Billy?" Billy's dad asked. "Did you have a fight with Tommy?"

Billy was too upset to answer so he just nodded his head yes.

"That's ok champ. It will be alright."

"No it won't," Billy said. "It will never be ok again."

"What's the matter buddy?" Billy's dad asked.

When Billy looked at his dad again he noticed the wrinkle that appeared between his eyebrows whenever his dad got serious. Billy couldn't say it so instead he just stuck out his hands. "These."

Billy's dad looked down at Billy's hands and found the right amount of fingers and  no scratches. In other words, it was exactly how eight-year-old hands should look. "They look like perfect little hands to me," Billy's dad said.

"That's how they look now," Billy said, feeling the need to cry again. "But soon they are going to be all hairy. No one else has hairy hands and I'm going to be the only one."

Billy looked at Billy's dad and the wrinkle again appeared between his eyes.

"Why do you think that?" he
asked.

"Because Tommy told me so,"
Billy said.

Billy's dad sat up, looked away as if
he was thinking and after a moment
stood up. Billy's dad then put his hands
on his waist and announced that the two
of them were going to walk to the park.

Billy liked to go to the park. And
even more, he liked it when he got to do

things with his dad without Tommy or his little sister Sam around.

When Billy got up, his dad stuck out his hand so that Billy could hold it. And even though Billy thought that he was too old to hold his dad's hand, he did it this one last time. Billy figured that soon his hand was going to be full of hair and no one would ever want to hold his hand again. He decided that he should get the hand holding while he still could.

2

"Hey dad, can I come with you?" Tommy asked as Billy and his dad crossed the living room.

"No, you're going to have to sit this one out, Tommy. This trip is just for me and Billy," Billy's dad said.

It made Billy feel good to see Tommy disappointed. And it made Billy feel even better that he was going on a special trip with his dad. Tommy was 13 and Tommy would say that 13 was too old to hold his dad's hand. Billy thought of this as a hand holding only trip. No other way was acceptable.

3

When Billy and his dad got to the park they took a seat on one of the benches. Billy really wanted to play on the monkey bars, but this time Billy felt like his dad wanted him to sit.

"So why did Tommy tell you that you were going to grow hair on your hands?" Billy's dad asked.

"I don't know," Billy said. But that wasn't the truth.

Tommy had actually told him that he was going to go blind as well. But Billy thought that his dad would be too sad to learn that he was going to have a son that was both blind and had hairy hands. Billy wanted to spare his dad the pain.

"Did Tommy say that because he saw you doing something?" Billy's dad asked.

Billy was amazed. Sometimes he thought that his dad knew everything in the world. "Yeah," Billy replied.

"Did he see you rubbing a part of your body?" Billy's dad asked again.

Billy was amazed again. "Yeah." But Billy quickly became worried, because if his dad knew about the curse, then it must be true. Billy looked down embarrassed.

"No need to be embarrassed, champ?" Billy's dad said lifting Billy's head up by placing his large fingers under Billy's chin. "Everybody does it."

Billy looked back at his dad's smiling face. Billy was confused. There was no way that everybody did it, because this was something he had just discovered in the shower.

He had been soaping himself when he had noticed that his privates  felt really good when he rubbed it. But after rubbing his privates a lot his body started to feel like he needed to pee even though nothing came out.

It had felt so good that he had done it the next night in the shower and then the night after that. It was then that Tommy saw him and told him that hair was going to grow on his hand and that he was going to go blind.

As soon as Billy heard that he went to his room to cry. Billy felt like a big boy, but the thought of hairy hands was enough to make anyone cry.

"What you did is something called masturbation, and every adult in this park has done it. And as you can see, none of them have hairy hands," Billy's dad said.

Billy looked around at the adults in the park. There was Mrs. Nelson, the mother of one of the boys in his school. There was Mr. Thomas who came to the park with his four-year-old daughter. There was Mr. and Mrs Wells, the couple from down the street. And there were a lot of other adults that Billy had seen but didn't know.

The thought that all of these adults had done what he had just discovered amazed Billy. And as he looked closer he also noticed that none of them had hairy hands.

"Did Mrs. Nelson masurbay?" Billy asked trying to remember how to say the word.

"Masturbate?" Billy's dad asked.

"Yeah."

"Well, everybody masturbates. So yes, that would include Mrs. Nelson."

Billy then spotted Miss Brooks, the pretty lady that his mom talked to in the grocery store. "Does Miss Brooks masturbate?"

"Miss Brooks isn't married, so I imagine that she does," Billy's dad answered.

"What does being married have to do with it?" Billy asked.

4

The wrinkle again appeared between Billy's dad's eyebrows and his dad looked away like he was thinking. When Billy's dad looked back at Billy, his dad seemed much happier.

"Our body is an amazing thing. Not only is it good for running and playing, but it is good for things that you can't even imagine yet.

Sometimes your stomach hurts and you don't know why. Sometimes your legs hurt and you don't know why. And sometimes your private parts become hard or swollen looking and you don't know why. All of those things happen so that one day you can grow big and strong and have kids of your own. That is the way our body is made.

And the way that adults have kids needs a boy's private parts and a girl's private parts. But if it didn't feel good to touch our private parts, no one would ever have babies. And because we all need family and friends, our bodies are made so that it feels good to touch and rub our private parts."

It made Billy feel good to know that Tommy was wrong. And a smile crawled across his face as he looked at all of the people that were like him. Billy then started thinking about his best friend Jack. He couldn't wait for the next time he saw Jack so he could share with him everything that his father had said.

"Are you thinking about telling your friends what I told you about masturbation?" Billy's dad asked.

Billy was amazed again. Sometimes he was also sure that his dad could read his mind. "I was thinking about telling Jack," Billy said.

"Do you ever talk to Jack about when you poop?" Billy's dad asked.

Billy laughed and said "sometimes."

"But you don't talk to everyone about when you poop, right?"

"No, that would be gross!" Billy said while squeezing his face into a twisted frown.

"Well, masturbation is like that. Everyone poops, just like everybody masturbates. But others don't want to hear you talking about your poops, and others don't like to hear you talk about when you masturbate.

Both are very important parts of life and both can feel good. But both can also make other people feel uncomfortable if you talk about it."

"Why does it make people feel uncomfortable?" Billy asked.

"Well Billy, boys and girls your age feel uncomfortable because you don't know what's happening or what's going to happen next with your bodies. When you don't know what's going on with your body, it can make you feel uncomfortable to talk about.

Boys and girls Tommy's age feel uncomfortable because they think that they are the only ones that are doing it, and it makes them feel uncomfortable to think that they are different from their friends.

Adults feel uncomfortable about masturbation because they think that everyone their age has stopped masturbating and that they are the only ones still doing it. But just like kids that are Tommy's age, those adults aren't the only ones doing it either."

"Tommy masturbates!" Billy said with surprise.

"Almost all boys at 13 do. Some girls may start when they're a little older, but they do it too."

Billy thought for a moment back to his baby sister. It was a surprising day when he realized that his sister didn't have a wiener like he did. Billy had asked his mom if his sister was missing one, and his mom had explained that that was what made boys different from girls.

But thinking about all of it now, he didn't understand how a girl could masturbate because as far as he knew, a wiener was very important to masturbate. "Daddy, how do girls masturbate if they don't have a wiener?"

"You mean a penis?" Billy's dad said.

"Yeah, a penis."

"Give me one of your feet," Billy's dad said.

Billy spun around on the bench and put one of his legs in his dad's lap. His dad then took off Billy's flip flop, took out the pen that he always kept in his pocket and asked Billy to look away.

"Did you feel that?" Billy's dad asked.

"No, what did you do?" Billy asked.

"I touched the heel of your foot with my pen. Ok, now give me your hand and look away."

"I felt that," Billy said with a smile.

"That is because there are things in your body called nerves. These are the things that allow you to feel when you're being touched.

There aren't a lot of nerves in the heel of your foot. But there are a lot of them in your finger tips. There are a lot more of them in your penis. That is why it feels good to touch it.

A girl doesn't have a penis, but she has something that has even more nerves than your penis. And when she touches that, it feels like it does when you touch your privates."

"Where is it?" Billy asked still confused.

"It is near where her pee comes out, just like on a boy."

"Wow," Billy said.

"And here is something that you should also know. When girls and boys masturbate, sometimes their private parts can swell a little afterwards. This is natural. It goes away in a few days and doesn't do you any harm.

And soon when you reach puberty, you will notice that after you masturbate, something sticky will come out of where you pee. This is natural for both boys and girls. It is an important part of how babies are made. And making babies is why masturbation feels so good to begin with.

When that stuff comes out, treat it like you would treat the stuff you blow out of your nose when you have a cold. You wouldn't blow your nose on your bed sheets or blow your nose onto the floor. And you wouldn't keep blowing your nose into the same handkerchief without washing it. "

"That would be gross!" Billy said.

"Exactly. So I expect you to use tissue or toilet paper to clean yourself off afterwards. And I expect you to be respectful to others who might not want to know that you masturbate. Can I count on you for that?"

"Yep," Billy said with a smile.

"Good boy."

Billy's dad got up to go and Billy stood up after him.

"Daddy, do you masturbate?" Billy asked.

5

Billy's dad walked back towards their house and Billy followed. Billy and his dad walked all the way to the sidewalk before Billy's dad answered. "Sometimes I do. But your mom prefers that I touch her in the way that married people do."

Billy thought for a second and then asked another question a little quieter. "Does mommy masturbate?"

"Billy, everybody masturbates or has masturbated in the past. Your grandparents have, your teachers have, and almost all of the kids at Tommy's school have. So yes, your mommy sometimes masturbates even though she might say that she doesn't. But like me, she would much prefer that we touch each other in the way that mommies and daddies do."

Billy and his dad walked a little further before Billy's dad continued. "As you get older there will be people who tell you that it's wrong to masturbate. And when that happens, you will have to listen to everything they tell you and then think about everything you know.

After that, you will have to decide whether or not you should stop. That is the type of decisions that you will have to make as you get older.

But I can tell you that cavemen used to masturbate. Even those people that have their pictures on our money masturbated. It is something that we all do.

But I'll say again, even though we all do it, it isn't something that we share with others. Do you understand?"

"Like poop, right?" Billy said.

Billy's dad laughed. "Exactly. Everyone poops, and everybody masturbates."

"Thanks dad," Billy said as he looked up at his father. Billy then slipped his hand into his dad's hand and smiled. He wasn't too old to hold his dad's hand, he decided. Maybe he would be too old in the future, but he wasn't too old today.

Grandparents masturbate.
Judges masturbate.
Even the lady down the street
masturbates.

Everybody masturbates.
Everybody masturbates! Everybody,
everybody, EVERYBODY
masturbates… or at least they will
sometime during their lifetime. :-)

The End.

Check out other books by
Cristian YoungMiller including:

Everybody Masturbates *for Girls*

'Everybody Masturbates *for Girls*' is the perfect gift idea for girls between the ages of 7 and 57 yrs old. Also, in the style of the classic book 'Everyone Poops,' 'Everybody Masturbates *for Girls*' addresses the specific issues that girls have accepting their emerging sexuality.

(It also makes a great party gift for adults.)